Whispers of the Heart

World Selected Poems

Latin Heritage Foundation

Latin Heritage Foundation

Whispers of the heart.

First edition.

© Latin Heritage Foundation, 2011.

All rights reserved. No part of this book may be reproduced, stored in retrieval system, or transmitted in any form or by any means, electronic, mechanical, photocopying, recording, or otherwise, except as may be expressly permitted by the applicable copyrights statutes or in writing by the authors.

Publisher: Gualdo Hidalgo.

Editor: Mariela M. Bonachea.

A Latin Heritage Foundation Edition.

Manufactured in United States of America.

For information, write:
ISBN: 978-0615531748

Latin Heritage Foundation.
8 Nunn Avenue, Washington, NJ 07882
United States of America
publisher@latinhf.com

PREFACE

> *"There's no money in poetry, but then there's no poetry in money, either".*
> *Robert Graves*

Latin Heritage Foundation is pleased to introduce readers to this anthology composed of genuine representatives of the contemporary art of poetry.

The authors are true poets. And not because they write poems. Anybody at some point in their live can write well, but in this particular case, they produce REAL ART that not only meets the formal parameters of the unit bottom-form, but comes to the deeper intricacies of the soul of every human being who loves the beauty of the word.

Their poems come from places geographically and culturally diverse as America, India, Nepal, Nigeria, Philippines, England, Canada, Israel, Jamaica, China, Bhutanese, and many more. And while not lacking in some specific locations of their creative evolution, after all, every artist is committed to its origins and roots, each poem shows a serenade of love and life, universal feelings, and however abstract, they are still the most important values as are the constant questioning of man's relationship to life and the vicissitudes that it offers. The poet does not live oyster locked in a tight under the sea, but is related to daily social surroundings that sometimes exceeds and even annihilates him/her. Precisely because of the acute sensitivity of their indomitable temperament, strong to poverty of spirit and ideals.

But rebelling against the long history maker of "accursed poets" (remember Arthur Rimbaud, Stephane Mallarme, Marceline Desbordes Valmores), the lucid writers who fill our ears with their musical rhymes in this anthology, out gracefully in every way.

The veins of these wordsmiths run the sap purest poetry. We believe it will be a real joy for the reader to enter in the pages of this must have book.

Reading and enjoyment of this work allows a better understanding of the world. The publication of the Anthology is also one of the best examples of The Latin Heritage Foundation interest to preserve, promote and disseminate the rich heritage and values of universal culture.

The authors, quite rightly, have earned a place in the book, because once, long ago decided to drop into the soft and networks indefinable poetry, literary genre sometimes confusing, sometimes vague, but carries however, both level of accuracy and knowledge of a language so much that sometimes trying to escape from its hands does not support poetry in any way. In it, you are, or are not.

We can only wish you to enjoy reading these beautiful poems. If this occurs, this will be our greatest satisfaction, and we will be more than rewarded

Gualdo Hidalgo
Executive Director
Philosopher, writer, screenwriter
Latin Heritage Foundation
United States of America
www.latinhf.com

Varun Amatya
Kathmandu, Nepal

I am originally from Nepal but currently I am an undergraduate BBA student currently studying in Assumption University, Bangkok, Thailand.

I am a day dreamer who seeks adrenaline rush and wishes of good things to happen for everybody in the world and I also believe in miracles.

I love travelling and I am not afraid of trying new things. I believe that I am a social person looking at the number of people I love to meet everyday in my university.

I have been writing poems for the last 7 years now and I have just recently started my own blog
www.varunwall.blogspot.com

Lastly about me I'd like to say that I am a person who loves life no matter what life brings because I understand that life cannot exist without bringing lemons in our lives so there is nothing to worry about because in future nothing matters so hence we should not be bothered by anything now..

My Olive Garden

My Baby So Pretty
Her Loves So Witty
My Baby So Nice
Who Can Never Suffice

My Baby So Cute
When She Act As Mute
My Baby So Hot
My Heart Is Her Spot

My Baby So Small
Catch Her When She Fall
My Baby So Tall
Enough To Join Varun Wall

My Baby So Sleek
Her Beauty Make Me Weak
My Baby So Slender
In Love I surrender

My Baby So Confused
My Love Got Accused
My Baby So Reserve
Only I Who Deserve

Neil Amber Patel
Chattisgarh, India

PERSONAL INFO: I'm a student just passed from high school 12th grade & currently preparing for medical entrance exam........
My parents are farmers.......I like to write poems to express myself...

Don't suppose me......

I m supposed to be strong & tough
to beat obstacles, that much hard enough...
I'm supposed to be gentle & kind...
to; leave gud impression, on everyone's mind
I'm supposed to beware of the lust,
to step a distance, form any kinda dust...
I'm supposed to work very hard.
Until catch up the so called goal, not to loose any guard........
I'm supposed to make, gentle & rich friends...
those with fake smile, even when shake hands.
I don't wanna be like any1's want...
i just wanna be myself, & do what i want...
I m not gentle, & neither strong
to suppose me being wise... they r very wrong....
Why to act tough & do hard work,
to act like a model, i m not that jerk...
I m not strong enough to raise my head,
I really feel lonely, also a bit afraid...

I m not that guy u want me to be,
i m just myself, what i need to be...
why am I supposed to be anything.....
why they wanna wake me up!! & cut my wing...
I can't understand the way they think ...
accept me just as me,, just another human being...

Miguel Barbosa Kortright
Guaynabo, Puerto Rico

Born in Puerto Rico. Young writer with hopes of a better future. Looks to inspire others to do the right thing and does not judge people by their cover. He is a listener and a problem solver. Mu favorite type of writing is psychological poetry. He has been writing since the age of 13, finishing his first collection of love poems while being 14 years old. I am aspiring to be an engineer and a life changer for those in need.

Inspired by: Pablo Neruda, Eduardo Barrios, and Salvador Dalí.

"You People"

I see my globe
consumed by whispers of pale blue,
a stained ground
by the wine of dismembered bodies.
Creator of screams,
plucking the very essence of souls
equal to your emotions.
You are Human.

Why judge when you yourselves
don't even know who you are?
Why accuse when so much more
awaits if we work as one?

Secrets you've seen in your lover's
sighs and stares.
Love consisting merely
in death, sorrow, tears.
Consumed daily by the fire of immorality...
You are human.

Are you willing
to be the agent that will destroy
all social boundaries?
Will you break free
from the oppressive nature
of addictions and filth?
You are human,
but I still have my hope
in the future we can create.

Tashi Gyeltshen
Bhutan

I am presently working as a teacher in Bhutan. I have completed my Bachelor of Education at the age of 23. Writing and getting pulished is my interest from childhood stage and my works include all round genres like poem, short story and essay. I have also been as the author of three books and I am currently working on the novel- "The wonder boy."

A Vow

Can you keep your head up while others put themselves down?
Since, you must raise when there is no loss of true pride.
Learn to choose when others choose by a chance.
And hold your strength too.

You can learn to defeat when others fear to lose.
So, your defeat will be the tribute-
Till you learn that losing is your prize.
For that- you must be fascinated by-
The dream of faraway returning ship,
When her sail is softly waving against the drifting wind-
That looked like a flag of permanent defeat.

Never think of if you can't, but be straight to hold it.
And it's your carpe diem plea which will let you;
Hear when they can't, see it while they don't.

Yet, do it while they just try to hear and see it.
And learn to retain what you have lost.

Raise your heart high while others are backed by otherwise;
Of sorrows, melancholy, greed, cunning,
And guilt for being pricked by-
Self-reproach, timidity and stupidity.
And take those matters for granted,
And be yourself a part of solution.

Prove yourself be working stoutheartedly, but even-headedly.
And always keep your heart opened.
Accept their views, but never quit-
To assure that you are beginning and doing.
I know-you will be defeated, but not destroyed.

Bunmi Orogun Olorunfemi
Lagos, Nigeria

Mr. Bunmi Orogun Olorunfemi Samuel a.k.a Yaro alias 'reality' was from a poor and greedy polygamist and bigamist subterranean miscegenation ethos background and was made a Lazarus himself and was also betrayed and treated with dared enviousness and jealousy of land acts use regardless his mission and vision to life art called. He married to a diverse matriarch misalliance religious politician woman who was from linage of a confused culture and made him a lovelorn and not a misogynist respectively. He was a Polytechnic graduate from Ogun State Abeokuta (Management Department) Nigeria. He was a Diaspora student in and at Yaba College of technology, Lagos, Nigeria and a scholarly member of a distance learning institute (DLI) university of Lagos, Akoka, Lagos state, Nigeria, Africa. He hails from auriferous city of Ikare Akoko in Ondo State sunshine city of Nigeria Africa and was proudly propped and grew beautifully at a mega city in Lagos state - Lagos State, Nigeria respectively. He attended saint Thomas Aquinas primary school Akinbaruwa Street Surulere Lagos, Nigeria and also, Atunrase Boys high school Owodele street off Ishaga road surulere, Lagos, Nigeria, and latter was transferred to Eko Boys high school Mushin, Lagos, Nigeria. Mr. Bunmi Olorunfemi Samuel was born on the third day of March 1976 at Ibadan town Oyo state Nigeria. He started his career first with U.T.C Aluminum department 27/29 Apapa Creek Road Lagos, Nigeria. In his fast growing ambition he found interest in acting as a profession. He passed through Pencils Film and television Institute 'PEFTI' and REMAX polytechnic Ogun State for advance course also on acting. He was meliorated to high level of arts called ' THE PROFESSIONALS ' by world known veteran Nigerian artiste in person of 'Mrs. TOYIN ADETUNMOBI' and the professionals was known fully well for its residential theatre performances at 10, Biadau Street off Keffi Road Ikoyi Lagos, Nigeria. He was from united ties of consanguinity of patriarch 'Dare Orogun' Christian Anglican family background like colleague veteran poet Christina Georgina Rossetti.

A REVISION OF A POET WHO DIED BY HIS POEM.

He is a man always left on his solitude,
with his might set, like a sharp sword,
His hands always exhausting pens,
with papers filled to the brim.

His heart gush and groan wide
with his head affirming, from side to side.
His words forces of wide thought
scheming words of all sought.

His dreams scanned in booklet,
this man rain all in droplet.
He exposes the secret of nature
and give details of all creature.

He mimics the ways of the philosophers
but not of vivid terms, it differs.
He writes of many immortal shadows
setting transparency of its immense sorrow.

His mind fight with his desires,
his heart embellishing what he has acquired.
When he turned activist of the state,
his works even the little hate.

His words read the heart of many
causing his plight to be plenty.
He was killed because of his poem,
He is an actor who died by his play,
A director who died by his directing,
A producer who died by his production,
A costumier who died by his costumes,
An editor who died by his editing,
A dancer who died by his dance,
A writer who died by his writing,
A banker who died by his banking,

A teacher who died by his teaching,
A medical doctor who died by his medicine,
A driver who died by his driving,
A drummer who died by his drumming,
A food seller who died by his food,
A browser who died by his browsing,
A carpenter who died by his carpentry,
A painter who died by his painting,
A noise maker who died by his noisy,
A pilot who died of piloting,
A computer operator who died by his computing,
Jesus Christ who died for our sins,
A poet who died by his poem.
He is a poet who died by his poem.

AFRICANS' BEAUTY

From a lullaby in cradle,
Where you glitter like marble,
To see your beautiful face,
They will know you come from a noble race,
I see tears in the face of the ugly,
That your beauty has erased,

You are of nice height,
And have skin like fine Gold,
Your hair solemn like the green grass,
Creamy for the touch of the morning dew,

I see beauty in your face,

I won't lie,
And even though I have to lie,
Not this time,

Looking at your face,
I saw spotless face that makes your face mingling with beauty,

When you walk,
You walked in such an amazing ease,
And give the earth a touch for peace.

When you talk,
I hear voice of a long awaiting sanity,
Because every of your words are benefiting.

When you touch me with your right hand,
I feel the touch in it like the morning dew that cools the blaze at night.
When you smile with your white teeth,
Radiating brilliance,
It looks like the gathering of an angels,
where white colors are found.
When you curl your stylish legs,
In such a profuse calling,
It clear to identify you,

This only,
The beautiful African woman.
This only,
The beautiful African Damsels.
This only,
The beautiful African Mothers.
This only,
The beautiful African Nation

Marvel Godwyn
Agbor, Nigeria

My name is Marvel Godwyn, from Delta state in Nigeria. I was born march 30th 1980 in my home town Agbor. I am a graduate of mechanical engineering.

A CORNERSTONE

See,
That stone
By nadir marred,
By murk furred,
By haze cocooned,
Like a straw
By gale of cruel fate buffeted,
By tongues of skeptics for eras
A meretricious folk christened,
By tunic of shame decked.
Like a serf, by dearth for
myriads of eras snared.

Has
By mettle
A pearl become,
By the hearth of cruel fate

A gold with a luminous light become
And nigh and distant tribes
On its ineffable glaring light
From the beset of darkness
Hasten to belay,
And their erroneous ethos
Their lips dither not to recant
For the stone, a cornerstone
Has become.

Anjali Mishra
Nagpur, India

I am Anjali Mishra, 13 years old, Modern School, Nagpur, India.

Summer Tempest

My love! May you be eternal,
If you are my dream, day should never dawn,
You are my goal, you are my terminal,
If you are my shadow, sun should never be gone.
If you are my hallucinations, they should never die,
If you are my swoon, I would never revive,
If you are my laughter, I would never utter a cry,
My soul, from you, I derive.
May you be like summer tempest,
That pours on me all the sorrows of thou,
You are a treasure I need to quest,
Every time- tomorrow, yesterday, and now.
You are my sadness, you are my glee,
Sweetest thou, I live for thee.

Kristin R. Schulz
Newton, Kansas

Kristin Schulz started writing at the age of 10. She is a sophomore in high school, where she enjoys managing football and boys bascktball. Also, she participates in the Writers Anonymous club where she can share her stories and poems with other students who love writing. Outside of school, Kristin enjoys playing the piano or violin; drawing animals and/or scenes from her small town of Newton, Kansas. She also enjoys spending quality time with her family and friends.

Missing Jammy Lynn

I am a deer, peaceful
And quiet, running away
From any danger

I am the grass, green, waving
Gently, inviting you to come
Enjoy the day

I am the creaky rocking chair,
Rocking in the wind, until
Someone comes for me

I am red like fire, glowing
ever So marvelously, but if not
Careful, I can burn you

I am an earthling, here to
Stay and help change
Earth if necessary

I am ageless, so young
At heart, yet growing
Older every year

Iyata Christi
Zephyrhills, Florida

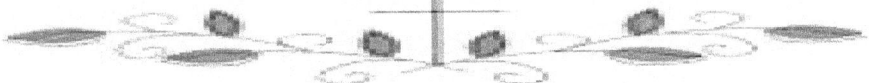

IYATA CHRISTI "WMNF; Caribbean Cruise Benefit Concert"

BIO:1) Iyata Christi is a misplaced Jamaican, who was grown in America. Her heritage is also influenced by, Spain, and Puerto Rico nationalities, yet she is mostly identified by her Jamaican background. At a very early age, Iyata's gift of expression was discovered through writing; now her works consist of Poetry and Lyrics, with books, and scripts in the making. In time Iyata discovered performing spoken word and currently Poetry, Lyrics, and Music are her top priorities! Iyata's signature at the end of all her Poems/works is *"ONE LOVE!"*

PHILOSOPHIES: 2) "Combining our gifts together we can achieve unity, equality, and justice for all of humanity." That is the inborn concept of Iyata Christi. Her natural ability to interject YAH/LOVE in everything, every time, anywhere, has assigned her the duty of being a Cultural-Spiritual Activist and Revolutionary. Iyata's gift is specifically created to encourage, enlighten, and heal.

3) Spoken word inspired through wisdom is always true prophecy! Live each day to the full, reaching for that better day that is promised and it must come! Living up, Stretching out, and Standing Strong is the new Black anthem! Together we must work to save Humanity, Our Earth, and All living life sources; it is our Duty for Our future Generations! ONE LOVE!

COLLEGE INFO/EDUCATIONAL JOURNEY: I am currently working towards my MBA in Marketing and then I will continue working towards my Doctorate in Philosophy.

Iyata Christi "Nature/Garden Photo"

Puerto Rican Pipeline
(*Puertorriqueño Gasoducto*)

Deceitfully, they want to run a deadly pipeline down the center of the entire length of the Puerto Rican island.
Using political puppets to spread their agenda…strings being pulled and maneuvered by the….
capitalist whoremongers! Destroying numerous life forms and ecosystems….while leakage pollution flows into all drinking….
water resources!

-The only sensible decision is….

Stop your plans for…. the Puerto Rican pipeline!-
-La única decisión sensata es….

Detener sus planes para….

el Puertorriqueño Gasoducto!-

What is the point of gas underground….

75 out of 100 miles long….
when there are many other sustainable options…. that are far more sound!
Your focus should be in the…. opposite direction….
Moving away from all dangerous…

gases, fossil fuels and deplorable....
mountain top removal intentions!
-The only sensible decision is....

Stop your plans for....
the Puerto Rican pipeline!-
-La única decisión sensata es....
Detener sus planes para....
el Puertorriqueño Gasoducto!-

You want to undercut a truly sustainable...
way of living....

by replacing it with unknown....
amounts of debilitating conditions! Remove your, "Love Dollars First,"
style of religion from before your eyes....
take time and listen to all of the most....
recent warning signs;...
dying life forms, irreplaceable ecosystems,
fresh water contamination, children born
with... physical handicaps and internal diseases....
The amounts of all these negative results....
will vastly grow....all the while....
your, "Loving money," ambitions of greed...

are clearly the only thing you see.... as
being something worthy to know!
When truly....

-The only sensible decision is....

Stop your plans for….

the Puerto Rican pipeline!-

-La única decisión sensata es….

Detener sus planes para….

el Puertorriqueño Gasoducto!-

ONE LOVE

IYATA CHRISTI

Xoaquima Carla Cristina Díaz
Miami, Florida

Xoaquima Díaz is a fiction writer and poet from Puerto Rico. A former journalist who published articles in Estylo, Latinos Magazine, Latin Girl Magazine and Latin Music Magazine, she is currently an Adjunct Professor of English at Miami Dade College. A graduate of Phillips Exeter Academy and Mills College, Xoaquima received her M.F.A. in Creative Writing from Antioch University. She served as a Contributing Editor for Story Quarterly and has recently completed her first novel, American Dreams, and her first collection of short stories, NeoRican. She has attended VONA Writers' Workshop several times, attended the Bread Loaf Writers' Conference in 2009, was awarded a three-week residency at Hedgebrook in July, 2010, and will be attending the first Bread Loaf Writers' Conference in Sicily in September 2011.

Flight 5401

I have never been afraid of flying
but a heaviness washes over me
when I enter the Mayagüez Airport
on Mother's Day, 2004
Something tells me not to board this plane
but practicality pushes me forward

When I arrive at security
realize I have lost my boarding pass
I know this is my sign
but the employees just laugh
send me back to the ticket counter
give me a new one

As I stand on the tarmac
waiting for them to board
the thirteen of us booked
on this 64-passenger flight
my stomach sinks
One by one
they place us on the plane

carefully distributing us
throughout the cabin
seat assignments ignored
to maintain balance in the air

Take off is uneventful
the half-hour flight
across my island is smooth
and I chide myself
for being paranoid

I laugh with relief when the captain announces
our descent into San Juan
follow both the sea and city with my eyes
always mesmerized by the beauty of home
la isla del encanto

Suddenly
we are dipping and swerving
There is no wind
no rain
no turbulence
but we are careening nonetheless
My heart stops
my stomach sinks

Screams of terror
frantic prayers
echo through the cabin

Papa Dios, por favor
ayúdanos

I see the runway
we are dropping way too fast
There is no question
I know we are going to crash

Screams of terror
frantic prayers
Papa Dios, por favor
ayúdanos

I grip my armrests
try to block out the noise
around me
and prepare for impact

Screams of terror
frantic prayers

Papa Dios, por favor
ayúdanos

We slam onto the tarmac
jolt and careen forward

Screams of terror
howls of pain
and frantic prayers

Papa Dios, por favor
ayúdanos

The pilot steadies the plane
as we rush down the runway
too quickly to stop before we
reach the ocean at the other end

Screams of terror
howls of pain
and frantic prayers

Papa Dios, por favor
ayúdanos

But we are on the ground
alive and intact
and I know we will survive
the rest of this ordeal
despite the

Screams of terror
howls of pain
and frantic prayers

Papa Dios, por favor
Ayúdanos

Suddenly
the plane rises again
the pilot pulls us up hard and fast
climbing skyward at a steep angle
like a rollercoaster creeping to its apex

Screams of terror
howls of pain
and frantic prayers

Papa Dios, por favor
ayúdanos

I stare out the window
numb with terror
This is the end
I am going to die

Screams of terror
howls of pain
and frantic prayers

Papa Dios, por favor
ayúdanos

The plane stops climbing
hangs suspended above the runway
then plummets back to earth
Screams of terror
howls of pain
and frantic prayers

Papa Dios, por favor
ayúdanos

I watch the ground rush up at me
an inventory of my life
floats through my head
timelessly
as I wait for death

Screams of terror
howls of pain
and frantic prayers
Papa Dios, por favor
ayúdanos

First anger
then sadness
Nobody knows I want to be cremated
half my ashes spread in the Caribbean Sea
the other half buried in Mayagüez
next to abuela.

Screams of terror
howls of pain
and frantic prayers
Papa Dios, por favor
ayúdanos

The plane smashes into the tarmac
my body whipped around like licorice

in a child's hand

Screams of terror
howls of pain
and frantic prayers

Papa Dios, por favor
ayúdanos

Darkness

I awake to screeching grinding noise
metal ripping and shredding
the sharp snap of plastic cracking

Screams of terror
howls of pain
and frantic prayers

Papa Dios, por favor
ayúdanos

The ceiling collapses on my head
shreds of black
fiberglass rain down

Screams of terror
howls of pain
and frantic prayers

Papa Dios, por favor
ayúdanos
Chaos continues
ceaseless
The plane does not stop
the screams do not stop
the flying debris does not stop

the crunch and grate of metal
on asphalt do not stop

Screams of terror
howls of pain
and frantic prayers do not stop

Papa Dios, por favor
ayúdanos

Darkness
again

When I awake the second time
the plane has stopped
but the noise hasn't

Screams of terror
howls of pain
and frantic prayers

Papa Dios, por favor
ayúdanos

We are in the grass on the side of the runway
The wing has been ripped from the roof
one end tilted up to the sky
like a greeting
the other jammed into the ground
in supplication
and still

Screams of terror
howls of pain
and frantic prayers
Papa Dios, por favor
ayúdanos

The propeller whines and whirs
digs into grass and soil
spits it back up at the windows
Noise and smoke and dirt
passengers and crew shouting nonsense
doing nonsense

Screams of terror
howls of pain
and frantic prayers

Papa Dios, por favor
ayúdanos

A woman behind me yells for a limousine
The man in front of me tries to push the fallen
broken pieces of the ceiling back together
The stewardess runs frantically in circles
like a headless chicken waiting to die
yells at us to stay calm

Screams of terror
howls of pain
and frantic prayers

Papa Dios, por favor
ayúdanos

The stewardess opens the door to the cockpit
sees the pilot's dead body
covered in blood and slumped over the controls
Her hysteria reaches new heights

Screams of terror
howls of pain
and frantic prayers

Papa Dios, por favor
ayúdanos

I have to get off this plane
before it explodes
I need to stand up and
open the emergency exit
But I cannot move
I am mute
immobile

Screams of terror
howls of pain
and frantic prayers

Papa Dios, por favor
ayúdanos

The other passengers scream
and jerk and twist in their seats
while I am silent and motionless
my mouth and body not responding
to the signals my brain sends them

screams of terror
howls of pain
and frantic prayers

Papa Dios, por favor
ayúdanos

Darkness
again

I awake to the shouts of rescue workers
They open the rear exit
urge us off the plane

in firm, calm tones

There is no mad scramble
people do not push each other
out of the way
do not trample each other
trying to escape
Everyone moves slowly, numbly
one by one
in order
rear to front

I am the last one
force my body out of my mangled seat
through the wreckage
toward safety

I jump down onto the asphalt
littered with airplane debris
and the final shreds of my sanity

Papa Dios, por favor
Ayúdame

Stephen Buoro
Minna, Nigeria

Stephen Buoro is a Nigerian, born in 1993. The renown Nigerian poet, Remi Raji, described his poetry thus: "This is the stuff poetry is made... [his] lines show the promise of a formative and remarkable voice...very innocent and lyrical." He is currently revising his poems for his first volume, Heaven Song.

I WILL FIND YOU

The stars have swirled to the nucleus of barbed guile

I remain the salience of their ridicule, left-toed stubbed,
Never to find or to be found!
I am the whirlwind
the earth is cliched of my fruitless wanderings.
I am the sun
with sporadic fatigue under my soles.
I am the moon
with day my bosom, in a duel with night;

Seeking for my dismembered being gifted with jinxes by the gods.

In the fruitful futility of my voyages,
I have ceaselessly cuddled the messiah
ardent to umbra alert eyes:
my flesh splayed by the Hydra of men
ravished by volcanoes, sheltering in the prison of ghouls
my being dawning as the rocky rebel of me…

And still not finding you…

In élan to melt in me
I will find you
on my molten parched pupils
you vowed.
You promised
to still persist as
the sun in my villi,
to dawn in your tongue-cremating glory
as my secondly coma,
to suffocate my ageless hemorrhage to healing,
to make me resurrect and dance on this sea…

Roost my
Goddess
Roost
Spring of radioactive ecstasy.

Like the mystique of seas' wombs to fishes
I want to hide in you and hide you in me
I want to melt in you and melt you in me
you the Avalon cataract of seaful thirst,
you're Lethe, the sore's source of smiles, the hunger of whirlpool ballets,
you, mother of seaful gropes to me for the celibate Elysian of days.

Roost my
Goddess
Roost
Spring of radioactive ecstasy
Save me from bleeding to a sour death.

And in this second, I will find and fill you.

AILY MEDITATIONS

"Knock, knock, knock!
Knock, knock, knock!"

Can't you hear me
knocking and knocking?
all these ages,
Child?
Has my knocking been so dumb
to rouse you?
Or have you been so deaf
to be roused?
I have been knocking and knocking
don't search so far away, Child,
don't stare at the standing still skies
or the effete mine of earth,
don't dive into the seas

or sprint in futility to the deserts.
Child,
I'm here before you, knocking,
knocking and knocking
on the daggered door of your heart.
Have you not been hearing
the honey, the Lethe, the Elysian
marathoning from my mouth?
I have been knocking and knocking
and will keep knocking
although my knocks grow grey hairs
and I have fallen to the mystery of Time,
now wizened.
Will you let me in?
Will you let me in?

I, the poison to your god of flesh,
the river to the fire of your heart,
the truth, the messiah to your dilemma,
the sole footpath to your horizon.
I, your everlasting beast of burden,
I have been knocking and knocking,
Will you let me in?
Will you let me in?
"Knock, knock, knock!
Knock, knock, knock!"

HAVE YOU SEEN THAT LAND?

Have you seen that land
where the perfect sun of ecstasy never dusk?

Have you dreamt of that kingdom
where grey hairs never grow?

Have you been lost in the coma of that heartland
where tongues never grow weary with their bulky, soulful songs?

Have you hallucinated of that city
where warmness brings to birth the drought of tears?

Have you found that spring
Where the coal of men could die and resurrect snow-like?

Have you foreseen that land
Of charring peace, where forgiveness suffocates?

Do you know there is a land
Where my whole flesh is for you?
Where I crave to crucified on your cross?

Will you come with me to this land?

Siddhi Kothari
Maharashtra, India

Footprints on the Sand of Time

Leaders fought for country
People fought for rights
Or a person comes in one's life
All have left their footprints behind
Memories sweet bitter or like lime
Have footprints on the sand of time

Like people comes and goes
Time too comes and goes
Somewhere there is felicity
And somewhere felicity's scarcity
Memories sweet bitter or like lime
Have footprints on the sand of time

One sits and muse
For such long-long hours
The footprints are like magnets
The memories are magnetized
Memories sweet bitter or like lime
Have footprints on the sand of time

Some paths have been changed
But not the memories
Life can make many turns

But something is left behind
Memories sweet bitter or like lime
Have footprints on the sand of time

Vera Berzak
Beer-Sheva, Israel

Born in 1987 in Russia and moved to Israel at the age of 3. Studies Visual Theater in Jerusalem.

Fragments of my Grandma

I am not sleeping, under my eyelids
A filmstrip is spinning wildly.
I am not still, under my skin
A flea army is marching.
Only these heavy bones,
Awake with ancient songs,
Redeemed with random memories
From a land now rarely known.

I see the thin-shaped child,
Riding on his bicycle.
The crooked road betrays his sight,
The flowering field stole his brown eye;

When down he falls,
he'll hide his tears
Behind his trembling back.

I'm not at rest, although the chest

Lays heavy as a stone;
Like a fowl who aims to fly,
But hardly ever soars. I
Remember fur coats in the storm
And the smell of hunger;
When shadowy men stood in the foyer,
They came for my own father.

Who
Slept with a suitcase near his bed,
As did any other.
Who
Did not pray before he crept
Underneath his blanket,
But hoped like every laborer
He would not turn unfavored.

'Do not tell', said my mother.
I was quiet as a mouse,
I grew lower than the grass.
But when they asked me why I cried,
Words rolled down like an avalanche.

The downtrodden woman
Who lived behind the wall,
Could not leave her house, with that
Snow piling at her door.
And he who'd been caught in Siberian tempest,
Would never walk at all.

We could trade tea bricks for money,
And buy our future dreams;
We could trust our neighbor's kindness, they
Weren't fond of hunting Jewish skin.

Okezie Hendrick Sage
Kaduna, Nigeria.

Born 44 years ago as the tenth child in a polygamous family of eighteen, in Umuahia South Local Government Area of Abia State, Nigeria, I was one of the stones the builders refused in that cruel and shallow trench where beauties and brains go down the drain.

Rejected by my father (who told me in clear terms that education was not necessary for me), I hit the streets at the age of 9 to fend for myself, with a view to satisfying my unquenchable academic desire.

Furthermore, I single-handedly educated myself in a public Library and refined my personality; dislodging the voice of pain and poverty to which I was susceptible, before I moved on with further studies.

As a plowman and a seed sower, trying to find the shape of my soul in the stone, my lush, green landscape of potential was first exploited in the nineties when I wrote series of drama scripts for Nigerian Television Authority (NTA's) "Drama Showcase", with hit titles like "Sweet Prodigal", "Tragic Revenge" and "Timeless Truth".

Having found my life's passion (Writing) and having continued to reexamine my deepest value (making a difference) - by introducing my revolutionary literary tradition to the world- my desires and affirmations to becoming a groundbreaking author has made it very difficult for me to rest content with conventionally accepted norms in writing.

RAGING STORM

The Veil of the night had given way

And the morning spreads across
The mountains of the great Effuzy,
Just like a ring of gold in the sky.

The blue sky birds singing their song;
The waves of the wondrous deep sea
Gently caressing the pebbled shores,
While the sunshine hid behind the clouds.

Feeling the wind of wider liberty
Blowing and blazing through my soul,
I was at peace; at peace with the world,
Lost in the rapture of a loving silence.

Sweet moments of endless peace
Tearing my heart apart with passion
With wondrous mysteries of life,
Hidden in the soft tendrils of nature.

Minutes after, the wind swept along
Just like an invisible turbulent hand
The waves crashed as loud as thunder
The storm stumbled in with great rage

The sea roared like an angry beast
Whose territory was just invaded,
Its tongue lashed the greasy shore
And like a trapped bird, I was taken

By the waters I was swiftly taken,
Taken in a dynamic state of motion,
Riding the tides with nothing left to hold
Except a rolling ocean, and the raging storm
'Is this life!' I said.
Losing sight of the shores, I discovered new oceans.

Lydia Suarez
Verona, New Jersey, United States

I am submitting for your review three poems from "Oxtail Memories" my memoir about my Cuban heritage as reflected through food and customs.

My stories and poems have appeared in publications including Prism Review, Mom Egg and Warren Adler Anthology.

E- zine credits include All Things Girl, Shine Journal, Apt., 971 Menu, Tuesday Shorts, and The Smoking Poet among other venues. A collection of my stories was selected as a finalist in the Grace Notes Discovering the Undiscovered Competition and my unpublished novel was chosen as a semifinalist for the Elixir Press Fiction Award. Work is forthcoming in Pearl and The Adroit Journal. Recently, my story Jersey Mambo was selected as a finalist in Glimmer Train's Short Story Award for New Writers.

Platanitos Fritos

"You fry bananas?" they ask. Americans who fear black spots
and covet skins the yellow of summer dresses,
Who are afraid of the perfume their skins emit,
hiding peels in the freezer until garbage day.
A coworker brings me his cheerio rejects, those left on a counter,
susceptible to the heat, turned like mafia informants.
"They're not bananas, their plantains," I explain.
The green ones are cut in chunks and fried in sizzling oil,
dripping dry on paper towels,
then smashed between brown paper bags during tough times,
or pressed in a paddle , fried again,
sphinxes,
eaten by passersby before they can be plated
crispy and so hot the salt evaporates on them like bathers in Miami beach.
Left unattended they will ripen,
but watched they are the proverbial boiling pot,
called *pintones*, not green enough to be *tostones*,
never ripe enough to be *platanitos*,
in the limbo of a day
darkened by clouds without rain and telegrams that never arrive.
The ripe ones are the dark brown of old piers,
 peachy orange inside, sliced lengthwise like slabs of minerals,
caramelized, sticky and tender to the fork,
fringed with bits of black licorice.
Platanitos, itos and itas, loving diminutives that we all are,
descendants of grandfathers and grandmothers,
abuelitos and *abuelitas,*
manolitos and teresitas,

platanitos,
sugar coated names.

Flan

The crossover dessert,
mispronounced to rhyme with plan.
More exotic than it's cousin crème brulee
temperamental as a soufflé
Quick to curdle, fall apart
a simple custard it is not.
Nervous ones show cracks in the foundation,
too bland, too pale, dependent on the pan
afraid of separation.
Those that are divine,
rise from the waters of *un baño de Maria*
varnished the orange of violins,
draped in velvet sauce.
The mortal ones a plateau
a jiggly monument covered in
freshly fallen coconut snow.

Café Expresso

La cafetera a suit of armour,
balanced on grates with perfect posture
before flat stovetops and dull coffee makers
water ebbing below the belly button bolt
black powder in the holster
brewing un cafecito
a thunderclap to the body.
Its phoenix beak open so we can see
when we hit the vein

the prelude a mysterious fragrance
electrifying the air,
a chorus signaling transformation
liquid dark as a well
rising mightily
defying gravity
black gold from a rig
leaving behind bubble kisses.

lanie Puyos
Quezon City, Philippines

Whispers of the Heart

The heart whispers to the wind
Blow me away, take me to the wilderness
Far, far away, where no one else has dwelt
In a place where I could swing and sway like feathers
And dance like fairies and fly like butterflies.

The heart whispers to the rain
Shower me, drown me into the ocean of dreams
Deep in my thoughts, where mind is at peace
And the soul escapes to wander around
Wanting to be free even for a moment.

The heart whispers to the sun
Brighten me, light up my way, lead me somewhere
To a world of wonders, where magic begins
Full of sparks, full of glitters
Leaving reality, never wanting to return.

The heart whispers to the sky
Hold me, as the clouds will carry me
In your arms of comfort, I shall be safe
Sleeping quietly, in your caring embrace
As you lullabye me tonight and forever.

The heart whispers to the star
I look at you, my one shining star
Take me now, and never let go
You are my light, my guide, and my shadow
For always, I will follow you.

The heart whispers to another
Close your eyes, touch your heart
Hear my words for they are true
Feel my heart for it is real
As I whisper I love you.

Safire Arista Lieurance
Fort Gratiot, Mi, United States

Jaded

With age comes unwanted knowledge,
and so develops my wish for ignorance.
My jaded eyes are burning with betrayal
and liquid hate. - How far idols fall
from their thrones when understanding plays a role.
Sewing the seeds of doubt
all hope is draining out,
Put back on the mask, candy coat the scene
I don't want to gaze upon the truth
When it's darker than the Shadows in me
My head aches with the stress of days accumulated
the anxiety threatening to overwhelm
But the ice cold air sears through the pain
a clarity only winter can bring
My tense muscles breathe in the chilled air
and relax under its frozen fingertips
My thoughts slow and each second
seems to be endless in this barren wonderland
Naked trees stand against the harsh dark sky
but a diamond embedded powder of white sparkles beneath my feet
Two beauties are at play here
on this chilled night
One of fragile innocence
and gentle touches
One of loss and pain
as Mother Earths creations wilt aw

Joanna Marie O. delos Santos
Philippines

The "Literary Queen", as they called me. I'm the former Associate Editor-in-Chief 2010-2011 of THE BLAZE, the official publication of Nueva Ecija University of Science and Technology in the Philippines. I'm currently residing at M.S Garcia, Philippines. The middle child among three siblings of Mr. Jovito and Mrs. Marita delos Santos. I finished my Bachelor of Science in Information Technology last April, 2011.

As a campus journalist, I've been a competitive person and have the passion in writing different articles like news, opinion, feature and most of all writing poems, short stories and novels. In my college days, I've been busy competing in different places in the Philippines with my forte "Poetry Writing" and "Feature Writing" in English language. Before being the associate editor of THE BLAZE, I started as a simple member of the publication being trained by seminars for competitions.

I won 5th place in Poetry Writing English in Regional Tertiary Press Congress in Region 3 entitled *"Somewhere I Called Paradise"*, and for the next year bagged the 2nd place in the same category, entitled *"O thy Waking Youth"*. After that year, I also won 10th place in Feature Writing category discussing the drug abusing my fellow youth.

O Thy Waking Youth

By: Joanna Marie de los Santos

It's thee, a youth of hope in light you move along
But why in gloom I found you dwells and know it's wrong?
The path you took, were twilight kissed the dark of night
And now you know what's wrong between the dark and light...

The truth is here to hug you in your deepest mourn
Have to wake! Sleep no more! Forlorn! Don't be in thorn
Please see the worth of thee and bestowed your sole self
Don't be alone or be disgusted to cheating elf

My fellow knows the truth to walk, beholds you
You wish of bliss but the solemn grief awaits you
Do not let the silence burst deep within your soul
'Cause lament heard from within imprisoned in your soul

It's thee, a youth of hope in light you move along
But why you're here in gloom again dwells so long alone?
I wish our life would be full of love more and more
To find the hope or soul hath been awake no more!

2nd Place in RTPC Region 3, Philippines
Balanga, Bataan
November, 2009

Nature's Serendipity

By

George Anne Brown

POETRY

North Palm Beach, FL, United States

George Anne Brown

George Anne Brown is retired actuarial analyst who has found a new interest in editing and eBook publishing.

Nature's Serendipity

Two tumbleweeds meet in flight
and dance to the fanciful antics of the wind.
Smiling in pure delight, they open their hearts
to rediscover a world in tandem.

Building momentum in an unknown journey,
Swirling in energetic joy, lightly touching,
they dart away to find each other again.

This time larger than before,
strengthened by emergent love,
they laugh at entangled differences,
dodge senseless propriety and deflect
conflicts of a confused society.

Fueled by passion to unite yet be free,
in a converging force, the tumbleweeds
are swept away by a confidence in ambiguity.

Finally caught by the grace of God's blessing,
they gently touch down until
tomorrow, when
reluctantly the tumbleweeds awake,
kiss softly, and bid farewell.

Michael Weidman
USA

My name is Michael Weidman. I am 18 years old. I am a student of Serra Catholic High School. I am a writer, a poet, and a songwriter. My writing can be as sometimes sad and uses nature many times for its beauty and similarity to other feelings and objects. I would like to write books and become a singer/songwriter. I want to have a positive influence on young people and help spread the Word of God.

Morning

Morning, yes morning, I remember well.
The burning circle began to rise.
Bird's call sounded like a bell.
There was always a surprise.

Whether it good or bad,
I discovered with the day's first word.
Still, the day never remained sad.
Of this, I was always sure.

Wild flowers gave their scent to me.
Neighbors greeted happy and aware.
Other children laid still asleep.
The world's troubles, I did not care.

Running through tall untamed grass.
Climbing a steep hill in bare feet.
Dashing home at parent's call, fast.
The days were always truly sweet.

The sky turned dreadfully dark.
The ball of fire extinguished from the sky.
Stars took their usual marks.
My hopes all went dry.

Love

Love, yes love, I remember well, so very well.
Years have passed by all too quick to count.
Knowledge has blessed me in such a large amount.
There's so many stories to brag of and tell.

No stranger could ever know my need for love.
To give, to receive, but charms were skills not gained.
Seeing others holding hands, kissing always pained.
Before returning to slumber, I prayed for help from above.

Though my eyes were clouded by feeling and desire,
Without these, I could still see her as nice.
Her mind, her body, her voice were stimulating ice,
But time would stop before she in me, admired.

My attention would be ignored and driven away.
Creating in me a torture of desire that remained.
Eclipsing the friends around when they came.
How could I tell them, what could I say?

As life's usual course, it ended with a friend.
Better that than a stranger in her view.
Yearning within a desire for love's sudden cue,
Yet no girl has come to rescue and help mend.

Dreams

Dreams, yes dreams, I remember well.
Screaming echoes touch upon my shell.
Trapped within a quiet, nice, warm cell.
Tales continue to find their way and tell.

An escape route to paradise awaited in bed.
Beneath the soft sheets, yellow and red.
I remember most of what is said.
Replaying moments long since dead.

A loving girl, beautiful and true.
Lingered about, but afterward, I knew.
A desire, unattained, nothing I could do.
Times always pull or push me to blue.

Strings and waterfalls may visit at night.
Making all things good except real life.
These shadows bring everyday work strife.
Something I could never win in fight or flight.

Now, few dreams pass by to greet.
No wonders or strangers to meet.
Just air about my cold feet.
As I lay restlessly asleep.

Death

An end? Death, I know well, oh too well,
A world of pain has haunted me too long,
Could there really be a solution?
One act that could break the cycle,
But only my suffering shall be hidden, not solved.
With it, creating sorrow across members of my bloodline,
Either way, the storm will find another to take hold.
Maybe they can fare better than I.

After years of searching for a partner,
My quest produces nothing, but experience.
The years remaining are as a hour glass,
Ready to drop its last grains at any date.

Its location remains a mystery.
No mere man can turn back all those years.
What would be the use of such feet?
What could I do different that I have tried?

A sharp knife, adoring my sad reflection.
No voice call to me to consider the act.
I have already pondered this and continue.
This very moment is just like my life,
Lonely, so lonely death seems a comfort.
A wasted lifetime, but to waste life?
Many before me pondered this,
But did any regrets their decision.

The sands are falling too slow for me.
Looking to the future, nightmares plaque my nights.
How much suffering can a man stand?
People speak of help, but where is mine?
So many see the desperation as I pass,
But no one stops to help.
They do not care for a stranger.
I no longer feel human anymore.

The reflection in the knife is that of fear.
Not of pain, but of death.
So many fear death,
Yet some never take time to think before it comes.
There is no reason to live,
And yet no reason to die except to escape,
But death will come with the falling sand.
I'll live until then.

Keagan Campbell
Ontario, Canada

My name is Keagan Campbell and I'm a 24 year old writer from Brampton, Ontario. I'm currently studying at York University as an English major with a minor in creative writing. Though I'm usually inspired by events in my everyday life, I more enjoy writing fiction and poetry more than anything else. My hyperactive imagination has always helped me in doing so and I hope to be able to entertain and inspire others with inventive and original stories the way I was inspired as a child. There is no greater joy for me than knowing someone enjoys my work.

Drown

By: Keagan Campbell

Your life preserver sinks me like a stone.
Its weight alone is slowly killing me.
For miles around I see I'm all alone.

No one hears my mumbles or my moans;
my screams are heard yet muffled by the sea.
Your life preserver sinks me like a stone,

Its weight – my sins for which I've not atoned,
I try to swim away but I can't flee,
And miles around I see I'm all alone.

My fate is something I cannot postpone,
the fates on high ignore my desperate plea:
"Those truthful words will sink you like a stone.

The life you had 'till now was time on loan
And now that time is up and you will see
the price you pay is to die all alone."

I grab your feet, then take the path I'm shown,
Beneath the sea to burry you and me.
Its your fault that I'm sinking like a stone,
so I refuse to just die all alone.

D. I. Ejuailo
Kaduna State, Nigeria.

STREAKING GREYS

In this, such a bitter time,
Craved in darkness, my soul
To Vanity, of a righteous blaze

Stamped by the quill of veracious sham
By a transvestite of ethos.

Behind the heart of darkness,
Mumbles pale light: resonating
In a sham of pious evil
Avidly, aided by the political beast
Whom, of today's serenade, is the piper.

Of nine demons, in orchestra
Conducted in symphonies by an angel
In an audience of precarious virgins
Through the night of red light, in vigil.
Cramming, to the understanding of day.

From sunset, in a mercurial line
Crinkling pounds, shambling dollars
Made spoils of ruling crowns
Sieving much, my derelict's worn
Of lost thoughts, to the vile of no villain.

Weening the academia
Of insight, and lost conscience
Pervading peace, for piles and pinches
In the jingles of a lousy tout
In this, a cunningness of louts.

In this time of distress of wads
And false decency in piety,
Seams wind to belligerent brotherliness
With a bout of disarray of history
To ineffectual mail, 'who gets what?'

To scums of the Earth in selfish stride
Jests and freaks, far and wide
Maim and mutilate, all in mide
As yet, unrighteous taughts stray untied.

Laura Sumler
Florien, LA, United States

I come from a Christian family. I am the oldest of four children. My parents taught us to live for the Lord. I was born and raised in the state of Louisiana, but now I am enrolled as a College student in California.

Christ Has Set Me Free

Rejecting Christ brought shame to me
I heeded not his plea,
But he still tried to make me see
I needed to be free.

But then one day I turned to him,
And he accepted me;
With arms of safety drew me in,
And now has set me free.

Now peace and joy I'd never known
He gives to me each day.
I never have to be alone;
He's with me all the way.

Aireen Grace Andal
Bulacan, Philippines

Aireen Grace Andal is a graduate student of Demography at the University of the Philippines. She graduated from college with a bachelor's degree in sociology last May, 2010. She is currently working as a technical writer and research assistant. She reads books on social sciences and humanities. Her favorite authors are Plato, Michel Foucault, John Braithwaite, Slavoj Žižek, Fyodor Dostoevsky and Leo Tolstoy. The Holy Bible (King James Version) is her favorite book. Her fields of interest are sociology of deviance, world politics, mortality, migration, child studies and comparative literature. She also engages herself in painting and reading manga series.

The Insult

As a picture blemished by words
The insult crushes a snake's head
Offends the merry soul, impedes a king's reason
Weakens the flesh and bones, difficult to ignore
The sunbeam ceases, the wood rots
In an empty dancehall, the moth dies
Swallowed by the earth's core, bruised
Unbecoming, poisoned, brutal, and drank
Cut, slain, burdened, ill
Eyes in motion, torn, worn and tired
To remedy, to ease is to cry
To wish for wings to fly and be gone
To rest, to regain sanity
To make little the once big
Invented by a dragon's tongue
To remember dignity, the soul once lost
To win the war, to refresh the spirit
To seek the soul, to fight the current
To rebut the ails, a self to remember

Augustine Oritseweyinmi Oghanrandukun Olomu (St.Ifa)
Sapele, Delta State, Nigeria.

BLOOMING LEADER
(Song for a real son of the land)

1. Bloom well in youth, lest bent age you deflower.
   The petals born of youth groom like strong tower
   Upon the flow'ry beds of our plum life,
   Bloom rich: a silv'ry song bred of rich fife.
   A new born day crows bold from panes of east;
   A new born life fills hearts with dainty feast.
   The flow'ry songs of noon blooms with sweet zest,
   Displaying love with all the petals blest.
   Like fair moon songs in a most happy night,
   Atose's colours beam with feathers bright.

2. Like a lorn mask that overstayed the shrine,
   Like an art work full stale that lost its shine;
   Like rare noon-moon that over used its lease,
   Like day-caught-owl that cants its hoots unease;
   Like morning Hespers of long forgot age,
   Our hungry minds searched for the hid sage,
   Like builders' bricks in search of safest coigns,
   Like full-blown pics limned bold in choicest coins,
   Like scalds of old that chant the songs of yore,
   We sought Atose to cure our grim sore.

3. We sought the bard to bail us from this bale,
   The bard, to cure our lobes from aching, pale.
   Sore songs were music to our doleful hearts,
   The sorry tunes that sold us at poor marts.
   Like fops caged in strange garbs we cursed the day
   Our clothes betray our beings like common prey.
   Sad grumpus of lost age, we breathe red fumes,
   Hot enough to crush feathers and rich plumes.
   Our fuming plumes were rays from house of Death,
   Grim Angel cruel that cuts all things of breath.

4. Before this time we basked at gate of wealth,
   Sweet jovial lizards, prinked in glorious health.
   Our poems rise, silent music of lorn soul,
   That sang the dirge that range from pole to pole.
   Our poems rise, joyous dinnings of great minds,
   That rope the hearts of greedy ones in blinds.
   Our poems rise, musings of prime fairest wit,
   Where wisdom great and sweetest songs do sit.
   Our poem rise, mellic songs of fullest hope,
   That bind capricious minds with angry rope.

5. Remember now, the days that slept with time -
   The memories of sweetest youth – your prime.
   We recollect the times cocooned in grace,
   When sun of dawn did breathe your promised face.
   St Patrick's joyed like lilies of bloomed May:
   You learnt, you prayed; you grew by night and day.
   Elume Grammar school came with noon-crown,
   A jovial school removed from baneful frown.
   Sweet butterfly at verge of richest spray,
   Unmoved by scorpions that attempt to prey.

6. Mere rustlers in game search; we combed the edge
   Of towns, we touched the souls of verdant sedge;
   We searched the richest wisdom tales of old,

Of tales unsoiled, from olden mouths foretold.
But truth like gold slipped by in grim passage.
The silv'ry hair of truth rings this message:
"Slow lazy pride is the Herculean glitch
We must uproot like weed to be true rich".
The echoes of St Patrick's, large like life,
Cure our inmost stale hope from bloody strife.

7. You journeyed much like zealous champ to win;
You paved the path of Death where sinners grin.
At last the summit smiles with rays of joy,
Rare rays that all our inmost fears destroy.
The gloamy sun of baleful wasted time,
Gives way to greener life of youthful prime.
I wish you were night-skies with myriad eyes
To scan your works blest full in jumbo size.
I wish you were the Saint with watchful ears,
You will save lobes from fear and baneful jeers.

8. The fireflies of the streets are wrought by you -
North, south; east, west – they fill over hungry view.
Our soles trail softly paths untouched by tar
Our feet sing bold, unstained by olden scar.
The scars of souls were mud of olden clime,
Moist, muddy mounts we groaned to scale and climb.
Eftsoons, the voice of man speak bold with fire;
You climbed, a saint with passions' full desire.
The fireflies of the street ring bold like gold,
Like gold of day that sings with passions bold.

9. Like glacier floe we swam your precious path,
Plum path of choicest love, unsoiled with wrath.
Base stars of fallen age scare you with tar,
A million stars will not the moon give scar.
Foul stars sang dins to swink the slinky moon
The fairest moon ignored their dinning croon.
Sweet heavens, sullied with fumes of rich dawn,

Bless us full with joys from verdant lawn.
Today, we move to end our piteous need,
Like birds to roost, we claim our rightful meed.

10. Now we come to the end of our rich songs,
We come to the end of the song of gong.
Like drowning sun that prowled its welkin west,
We drown our fears and seek the path of rest.
To the extreme of our rich tunes come we,
With Popish pride to tame our happy See.
We rued the day we toed the lane of lies.
We curse the days of ooze and hideous flies.
We come to the verge of our soulful tunes,
The jolly path of Godwin's mystic runes.

Martha Guadalupe Solís de la Fuente
Coahuila, México

My name is Martha Guadalupe Solís de la Fuente. I am 17 years old and i live in Monclova, Coahuila, Mexico. I love to write essays, stories, articles, and I especially enjoy writing poems. Writing for me is the best way to express feelings in a way that only the reader can flow in that magical road of imagination, intuition and can travel to a world where there is only passion and feelings. Last April I went to Oaxaca Mexico, where I won the 2 place in the ¨PIBA¨

International Poetry Contest in which I wrote "The world from my eyes" and I performed it. I have been writing since I was 15 years old and right now I have several pages on word of different kinds of writings. I hope you enjoy my poems and you understand what they hide inside every word.

Wait, What?

Wait what?
Yeah that was my reaction
Not my intention
Just my emotion

Thanks, thanks for being yourself
Being selfish
Thinking just by how you feel
And not by how I did

Thanks, for showing me words of wisdom
Words of love
And the way you hug me with your arms
And the strength you had
Let me tell you,
I believed you.

Let me tell you,
I was hurt by you.

It's not over
It's not
But wait what?

You said the same, exactly words to her, that to me?
Are you happy now?

Do you realize what you've done?
What have you just lost?

I don't think so
Let me show you
What I can be NOW

But wait, wait what?
Yeah, I'm fine thanks,
Thanks for letting me go
With a better man.

With one that can really love me
One that can really tell me the truth
One, one day I'm going to find LOVE.

And wait what?
I never thought you were that kind of guy
I never thought you, yeah you, would break my heart

I'm an angel

Outside the sky is crying
I already did
I lost a battle, but not a field

I have touch the ground,
But I'm putting on my wings
I lost my way
I'm just standing here

I came here to look for love,
But love wasn't looking for me
So far I'm just standing here
Okay I think I'm a little further now

He said, the eyes of a person are the doors of the soul
Once it looks at you
It opens out
I'm an angel I felt from the hands of God,
So where are you now?

Oh dear soul, with or without wings
Let me go fly, lend on me
Because I know I didn't fall from anything,
I know I have a destiny!

My first boyfriend

I think it was on February
When I met an awesome guy
Who did a little "rary"
And then he broke my heart

I thought he was my boy
Who came into a point?
I realize I've never felt
This way before

We went through movies and dinners
We had a lot of memories
And at the end you decided to cheat on me
With a girl I used to see you with

You can go ahead and have fun with her
While I wait until it's May

Maybe we weren't meant to be
Or maybe we were
But you know that at the end
You'll always be my friend!

In the middle of nowhere

I would rather sleep
Than to say all my hopes, my dreams
Unnecessary I intended to be someone
In someone's arms, in someone's life
But I never realize I already was

I couldn't hide my intention of writing
But at the time I notice, I was a writer
Blue or white, orange or apple
So many words
But they're almost the same

Created in a book, born in a paper
How can they expect me to write more with those?
If for me, you ask
I cannot tell you the truth

Because as our feelings grow up
So do me,
¿So do you?

I'm not caring for grammar anymore
For it, it will eventually change
But the feeling through the years
Remain the same

I always wanted to leave
But I found that I've already left
I was never here
You are where your mind is
So don't try to change that please
Silence down your speech or someone will hear it
Let them copy your happiness, but let them always wonder

I stayed, because they put me in

Long years of my life
Using wigs, using bars

One day when I got too tired
I tried to get the sleep forever
Not because I wasn't clever
But because I was

So I got in bed,
And then got up at 10
Because I cannot sleep, while the world is alive
I cannot let go this opportunity
The opportunity of life

Live to leave

For life is, I have no kingdom
I have travel all my life to see the sun
I don't have much to talk about
But at the time I met you I knew

That I could cry forever
And I can surround my soul of sound
But I had never felt the fear of leaving

Where my steps could be implanted
And my mind could live in peace
Thou there is no way to look back
Thou I have nothing free
The ager killed people along my road
In which I remember, my best friend
No one is here to live

The hate for her had left the piece

The greatest women, with awesome minds
Have left to grandeur this old comfy town

To follow a star or to follow a dream
Let my words go inside of me
And my feeling never escape because of someone
And someone not be

Unspeakable words in crazy heads
Powers wanting to born in the middle of nowhere

I tell you my friend,
Live to leave before they speak
Live to leave because there will be a time where everyone will be together
Together in a better world

Live to leave the town where there is no happiness
For you, you are alone to decide
You only live once

The sparkly revenge

That tiny, little thing called nail
Placed in my feet
Stayed with grime
Oh mama told me to clean it up

¡But I didn't!
I forgot to
Now my nail is
Well, you can say it is black & yellow

Black at the top, at the bottom it is hard to see

This stinky and smelly foot of mine
I bet you, one day, you're going to die

But while you're on my hands
I'm going to make what I can
As far I am concern
You're the one that make me walk away

So here you are in front of me
On my right side the pool
On the other my orange flower flip flops
Manicure pedicure
Tell me what's the cure?
Should I stay pink, or should I pick blue?

I'm going to suck off the dust
Leave you clean
Wanting to shine on
Telling the people you're ready to go!

It is 4 o clock
And summer's here
My friends they got tattoos
But I rather go to sleep

Those queen naps I take
They make me feel great
They're going to make the wrinkles go away!

Come on, it is 5 o clock and we ought to focus
Where was I?
Oh yeah!

Let's start with the basic
Nail clippers
Then filing my nails
And at the end, the sweet revenge

Some sparkly polish

Oh my…
You look fantastic!
See, I told you I wasn't going to hurt you
Some perfume here
Some water there

And I can finally see
What it is to have a clean nail
Just remember girl
Always be on top

But to get to your hopes
Be careful with what you are walking on!

Paola Luz R. Tolentino
Manila, Philippines

In the Street

Here in the street,
it is very common, to see a…
running office man,
walking runners,
cars not driven
and sellers selling anything.

Here in the street,
it is very funny to hear a…
nonsense chatters chatting,
loud speaker for attraction,
noisy drivers driving,
and the latest about everything.

Here in the street,
it is also very popular the…
preachers in the morning,
and the crimes at night.

But, one thing is unnoticeable,
here in the street,
is the beginning and the end
of our journey…

Christina Marie Sloss
Houston, TX

Familiar Foreigner

Familiar foreigner of my bed,
Together we lay between two worlds apart
Separately dreaming, yet intrinsically one
We physically intertwine and spiritually connect, yet at times are linguistically divergent.

Two states without borders
We're two minds running in different orders
Weathering each other as we begin to mold our lives towards together

Needing independence
Keeping individuality…
Yet constantly seeking togetherness

Leigh Anne Cooper
Rio Rancho, New Mexico

Having grown up in New Mexico surrounded by the intriguing open land of mesa and mountains, I enjoy spending most of my time hiking and exploring the area around my home near Albuquerque. I am currently a student at Colorado State University studying Equine Science and English with the hopes of going into journalism or something of that sort.

The Rio Grande

You can hear the wind; it's lapping through the trees now, sending a ripple, a gentle tap-tap-tap of the leaves. Almost like hearing the rainfall without getting wet.

Some of the leaves are dead and under foot, crunching away with each foot fall, sounding your progress down the empty path.

A few birds swoop by, the woosh of their wings seemingly swoop right by the side of your face. Only one chirp and they are gone, diving to a new location.

You made it the sand, slipping and sliding you stumble forward, struggling to keep the pace with the muffle thump, then slide, sink, grind.

It's quieter than before, no trees to cover you, but instead the tall weedy plants on either side, dried and tipping. There is a rustling; is it the breeze or something else?

Babbling of water hits you. Follow and it only gets louder. The faint lapping on the edge mixed with the steady shhh of the water in the middle.

There's a solid blub next to you; a stick is stuck in the mud while the water hurries to go around. Something else is stuck, but you can't hear it.

You can't hear the color but you know it's brown, muddy, thick. The water blocks your path and you're stuck. Only the river gets to move on.

Jasmine Suzana Valdes
United States

There's not much to my story. I'm a senior in high school just trying to find a voice. I have loved poetry for as long as I can remember. Most of my poetry is not based on my experiences but rather of those that I love and care for. Though I'm young, I seem to be the person people confide to, and when their story moves me I get inspired to write about it. Other times I write a poem to comfort my friends and family that confide in me and though it seems insignificant at first my poetry really helps them overcome their hardships. I'm an opened minded person, but complex as well. Writing poetry always helps me think about a situation from more than one perspective, and being a teenager surrounded by peer pressure and confusion on life in general, it really makes a difference on how I make decisions and chose to live my life. I hope to be a published writer one day, but in the end poetry will always be apart of my life, even if I'm not acknowledged for it.

Strength Within

Did you see the hope in her eyes,
or were you blind then too?
Can't you see the hurt in her eyes,
as she says "I love you"?

Who are you to tell her what she feels,
and who are you to deny her beauty?
When it's her love you steal,
and it's pain she feels completely.

But what can she do?
She feels lost without you.
Your that something she holds on to,
and you abuse it and take her as a fool.

One day she'll see the errors in your ways.
I just hope its before its too late.
She'll stand tall and have you begging at her feet,
then she'll walk away to show you she's not weak.

And who is she?
She is we.
We all have that strength within us,
just waiting to be free.

Nehemiah Wong
Shenzhen, P.R. of China

Nehemiah grew up in the region called South-East Asia. So that at an early age, he had absorbed a multi-culturalism which is richly diverse.

English wasn't his mother tongue, but it was the official medium of his education. He was a passionate young reader; but when it came to writing, he struggled with an art demanding perfection.

Though baffled he never stopped relating to English as an integral part of his life. He first started his professional career as a young writer, scribbling for a men's magazine.

Later on he studied theology which exposed him to many important branches of human knowledge, including: archeology, semantics, linguistics, philosophy, psychology and rhetoric.

He then stepped into his second career choice, caring for communities in the region. But more recently, having reached a chronological milestone, he has again an urge to write creatively.

He's now musing on the charming discovery, how life can come one full circle without intending. That no matter, how far one has advanced on the timeline, one can't fully escape from the pull of his or her roots.

Nehemiah is happily married and is an Australian citizen, residing in a suburb of Melbourne. Presently, he is working overseas in China, with his devoted wife and companion, Grace.

THE SENSE OF TIME

When questioned...
TIME stood still,
and was mute!"

"Answering only with
the irony of silence."

Then a voice in my ear whispered,
And in startling manner chided.

"You ask for your youth back.
 And for time to rollback."
"But can rivers flow upward?
Or leaves sprout downward?"

"Neither can TIME,
be childishly tampered!
Else, Reality will
Forever, be scrambled."

"You ask for me?"
But I've been with you,
the whole time!"

"Shouldn't you've known?"
"The tree's in the sapling,
And the sapling, in the tree?"

"For I am but that
inner child,
of your past. "

"And you're but an offspring
of Time: a triune being."
An interlocking of beings

unlocking in a three fold
Universe.
"Interacting organically
as one:

As a child of the past:
a stalwart of the present:
and a voyager of the future."

"Each, in his own time and space:
"a three-fold cord which cannot,
be easily broken."

"So embrace this
sense of Time, O!
you offspring
of mystic Time:
for you're
wonderfully
made!"

Nehemiah K.H. Wong
©2011-6-12

HOMELESS WOMAN"

Homeless woman without a soul
Sleeping outside in the cold

Clutching her dirty raggedy pillow
Swallowing lumps of bitter sorrow

Closer to her breast her pillow pressed
As if, her living daughter, she caressed

The cruel wintery wind begins to jest
Freezing both with its icy breath

Her grimace, on the face, will never show
For her soul has been numbed by many blows

The screams, you can only hear,
If you have a ricocheting ear

©2011-2-4

"THE METAMORPH"

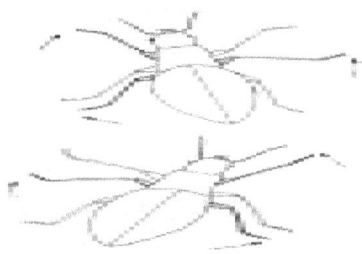

Wouldn't you
scream yourself
silly, if you
should awake
one morning
to find yourself
turned into a
"Metamorph?"

It's not a
laughing matter
at all
if you did.
No, not at all.

It wasn't for
Gregor Samsa.
Wasn't funny
at all for him,
to find himself
turned into
the biggest of bug,
one dubious
morning.

Lying
helplessly,
he saw his:
many
tiny
legs,
kicking
in the air,
flicking
in the air.

On his

horny back,
he was
horrified
to see
his segmented
domelike
belly, in bed.

After this
he was
completely
out of sorts:
and couldn't
even lift himself
from his bed,
to face the
grotesque day.

"Who done it?
Who done this
cruel deed to
Gregor Samsa?"
A jolly good
fellow by all
accounts.

Well, as it
turned out,
it was
Franz Kafka, a
"Metamorpher,"
a conjurer
with the power
of potent words,
who done it!
Done it with
his magic pen.

He dribbled some
funny ink and
wove a darkish
spell, from a
nightmarish hell,
for Gregor Samsa.
That's right,
he done it!
Franz Kafka
done it!
to the harmless
bloke.

And why did he
do it?

Pain and torment!
I reckon are the
plainest reasons.

For so it's
widely rumored
that such eccentric
souls are often
bedeviled by a
writing distemper,
they called the
"poetic license,"
and through this
mode of
projections,
find catharsis
and palliation
for their own
agony.

Perhaps, on this
account, sensitive
Hamlet couldn't,
and wouldn't,
sleep just so!

For he was afraid,
"That in that sleep…
where there's
no return…what…
may come?"
at the hands
of these
peculiar ones.

Therefore he
often pondered
the question:
"To be or not to be?"
A vexatious
conundrum,
to keep himself
from drowsing
and slumbering.

And not only
for him, but
also for all
kindred
souls
down the
sleepless
centuries.

Chanting,
"To be
or not to be?"

between our
blankets,
with wide-eyed
wakefulness.
Fearing ourselves
hideously changed
by some nocturnal
transmutations.
Nervous of finding,
in the morning-light,
we've become
Frankenstein-like.

Poor noble Hamlet,
Shakespeare made
him into an
indecisive
insomniac…
unraveled by the
tragedy of fear.
But a great and
princely soul
he nevertheless
was before he
"metamorphed."

And that's what a
"Metamorph"
truly is:

Which is any
human being,
becoming a
gigantic bug,
or one with
a donkey's
head, or even

just being a
plain mega moth,
or anything
less than
what our
Maker
intended
us to be.
©2011-6-16

SONG OF THE CICADAS

After the Spring rains had freshly
fallen, and the ground softly sodden,
the long imprisoned cicadas awake
from their cryonic chambers.

They pry free from their dark
subterranean prison and march up
the nearest trees. They head for the
dazzling tree-tops: and on secure
perches, screech lustily, from tree to
tree.

Their saw-buzzing shatters the cold
quietude of our starry blue nights.
The cacophony stabs our ears, and
steals our peace.

But to the droning throng, it's the
sweetest siren song.
The rite of passage, from generation to generation,
till the fading of time.

Aren't these songs and rhythms
indexes of meaningful design?
Visible thumbprints of an invisible
Deity ?

Did not an ancient text say, that
the "stars sang out together with joy"
at the dawn of Creation? Stars or
cicadas, are they not similar jubilant
sparks or molecules forged by the
hammer of the same Maker? © 2011

<u>Background</u>
This phenomenon took place after a
heavy Spring storm in China. The
disturbing but intriguing noise is a
mating and death call. All the cicadas
will die after mating: the males almost
immediately after their frenzy and the
females soon after dropping their
eggs.

LONELY SWIMMER

All along the River Pearl, its water flowed like smooth oil-rolls. Here the bum-boats chug and water-hyacinths are plucked.

And from afar is spied, the bobbing white cap of a lonely swimmer, lunging hard against the mighty River.

Whipping rains arose and lashing tides intimidate : but the plucky swimmer with steelier faith forges ahead.

What banshee would drive someone to battle this juggernaut? To gamble body, soul, and all, at a dice's throw.

But then, aren't we in comparable circumstances and constraints caught? Aren't we with similar frightful paradigms wrought?

Cast out as it were, by birth, from
origins unknown; unbidden,
unprotected, unenlightened into this
forbidding river of life: facing
greater odds of danger with nowhere
else to go or hide; wrestling ceaselessly
with the forces of time, of
chance, of nature, of dangers unknown; driven
nakedly, as it is, from a safer Paradise,
only to wander in a wilderness of
rocks and tears.

In this "Game of Life" none can
refuse to play. For the pangs of
default would be the worse: in letting
forces random to blindly forge our
destiny instead.

For whoever we are, and wherever
we are, we must acquit ourselves as
men. For how do we know, if we
aren't, by petulant omission,
squandering, if there be, all, or any
future glory stored ahead?

Elizabeth Wesley
Ontario, Canada

June

The languid eyes of soft sleepy June,
Awaken to tease the flowers that bloom;
With liquors of dew for striped honey bees,
Dipping their straws if the blossom agrees.

Let the whispering wind fly with no haste,
Thro pavilions of blossoms dotted with lace;

Where tender feet trip thro the myriad of greens,
To paint the pastures of June's sunny scenes.

The ancient forests deck far away hills,
Where winding streams drift thro unruly rills;
And the alchemy of all that is told,
Turns mossy stones into precious gold.

The perfumed petals adorned with scent,
Surround everywhere the elfin spirits went;
As these little ones skipped thro the sunlit day,
It was with these shadows I needed to play.

So the chapter of June comes to a close,
She floats into summer on the scent of a rose;
She pirouettes on tiptoe in her gossamer gown,
Wearing on her head a bright golden crown.

Annelie Nghikembua

I am an aspiring poet. I have written two anthologies of poems. In 2005 I won the first prize in the poetry competition sponsored by the National Institute of Democracy (NID). In 1994 I became one of the top ten finalists for the short story writing competition, KTV-South Africa. In 2006 I won in the essay competition in SADC under the theme "Speak Africa" and was appointed to partake in the speak Africa media coverage sponsored by Unicef-Africa in Ethiopia. I have written a play too, which at the moment isn't published but still in the editorial stage. I am a holder of an honors degree which I obtained from Rhodes University South Africa in 2009, my majors were English and leadership and management. I obtained my first degree from the University of Namibia in 2004 specializing in English and Economics. Presently I am working towards a master degree in Linguistics. I am a teacher by profession, and teach English as a second language-High level. Through my years of teaching, to be exact for the past four years I have received awards for being the best teacher in the region and for maintaining a hundred percent pass. Writing is my passion and I am hoping to be an acknowledged writer one day.

Imagination tainted

I recall thy love as precious and true.
In my shattered mind, some memories go
Your humor lingers, that smile mistaken
Shall I not. Beds of rose pour me again
Red sweet berries spread like leaves of spring
To the ground they lay, love I'm waiting.
Behold your words as diamonds sparkling tone

On this page emotions placed...tis my zone
Your silence eats my bones and my dearheart
Darling couples ought we been. Alas! This hurt
An open caring, kind heart shall I tell,
Of this deep true love memoirs, pain Ikept,
Let the dove loose, for it may perch oneday.
Now you know the pain and burden kept in

CONTENTS

Varun Amatya, Nepal/ My Olive Garden	/5
Neil Amber Patel, India / Don't suppose me...	/7
Miguel Barbosa Kortright, Puerto rico/ "You People"	/9
Tashi Gyeltshen, Bhutan/ A Vow	/11
Bunmi Orogun Olorunfemi, Nigeria	
*A revision of a poet who died by his poem	/13
*Africans'beauty	/16
Marvel Godwyn, Nigeria/ A cornerstone	/19
Anjali Mishra, India/ Summer Tempest	/21
Kristin R. Schulz, United States/ Missing Jammy Lynn	/23
Iyata Christi, Jamaica/ Puerto Rican Pipeline	/25
Xoaquima Carla Cristina Díaz, Puerto Rico / Flight 5401	/31
Stephen Buoro, Nigeria	
*I will find you	/43
*Aily meditations	/45
*Have you seen that land?	/46
Siddhi Kothari, India/ Footprints on the Sand of Time	/49
Vera Berzak, Israel/ Fragments of my Grandma	/51
Okezie Hendrick Sage, Nigeria/ Raging storm	/53
Lydia Suarez, Cuba	
*Platanitos Fritos	/55
*Flan	/57
*Café Expresso	/57
lanie Puyos, Philippines/ Whispers of the Heart	/59
Safire Arista Lieurance, United States/ Jaded	/61
Joanna Marie O. de los Santos, Philippines / O Thy Waking Youth	/63
George Anne Brown, United States/ Nature's Serendipity	/68
Michael Weidman, United States	

*Morning	/71
*Love	/73
*Dreams	/73
*Death	/74
Keagan Campbell, Canada/ Drown	/77
D. I. Ejuailo, Nigeria/ Streaking greys	/81
Laura Sumler, United States/ Christ Has Set Me Free	/83
Aireen Grace Andal, Philippines/ The Insult	/85
Augustine Oritseweyinmi ,Nigeria/ Blooming leader	/87
Martha Solís, México	
*Wait, What?	/91
*I'm an angel	/93
*My first boyfriend	/94
*In the middle of nowhere	/95
*Live to leave	/96
*The sparkly revenge	/97
Paola Luz R. Tolentino, Philippines/ In the Street	/101
Christina Marie Sloss, United States/Familiar Foreigner	/103
Leigh Anne Cooper, United states/ The Rio Grande	/105
Jasmine Suzana Valdes, United States/ Strength Within	/107
Nehemiah Wong, China	
The sense of time	/111
Homeless woman	/114
The metamorph	/115
Song of the cicadas	/121
Lonely swimmer	/123
Elizabeth Wesley, Canada/ June	/125
Annelie Nghikembua/ Imagination tainted	/127

www.ingramcontent.com/pod-product-compliance
Lightning Source LLC
Chambersburg PA
CBHW031402040426
42444CB00005B/387